Original title:
Ripe for Romance

Copyright © 2025 Creative Arts Management OÜ
All rights reserved.

Author: Thomas Sinclair
ISBN HARDBACK: 978-1-80586-276-5
ISBN PAPERBACK: 978-1-80586-748-7

Caressed by the Lavender Wind

In fields where that scent floats by,
The bees don't just buzz—they sigh.
With each petal, a flirty tease,
Even the flowers sway with ease.

A bumblebee wears a tiny hat,
He's the life of the garden, imagine that!
The breeze whispers secrets, oh so sweet,
While squirrels put on tiny ballet feats.

Moonlight Hits the Orchard

The moon wakes up with a chuckling glow,
And apples blush as the shadows grow.
A pair of raccoons start a dance,
They twirl 'round trunks, oh what a chance!

With cider dreams beneath the stars,
They toast with acorns, filled with jars.
Those owls are really quite the crowd,
Hooping along, feeling quite proud.

Apricot Dreams and Wildflower Paths

Apricots dangle and wink like friends,
Telling tales as summer bends.
Wildflowers giggle, spread like cheer,
"Don't trip on petals, or we'll disappear!"

In the whispering breeze, a soft surprise,
A clumsy deer with big, silly eyes.
He stumbles and fumbles, a comedic sight,
While daisies chuckle, oh what a night!

The Lattice of Longing

Twinkling lights through the garden gate,
As fireflies buzz, they flirt and sate.
The vines interlace, a love-yarn spun,
What tangled romance, oh isn't it fun?

A frog in a tux, he croaks a tune,
Dreams of a dance beneath a full moon.
The crickets join in, with their own little jam,
As laughter echoes, what a wee sham!

Dappled Light and Tender Glances

In dappled light, we sneak a peek,
As laughter floats, it's quite unique.
You trip on air, I spill my drink,
Our love's a mess, or so we think.

A glance exchanged, the shyest smile,
We dance like fools, yet all the while.
Your cheek's a canvas, painted red,
I might just kiss you, if you'll tread.

The Lengthening Shadows of Desire

As shadows stretch across the floor,
Your laugh is loud, I can't ignore.
We chase the dusk, like kids on bikes,
With whispered dreams and silly hikes.

The moonlight casts a silver glow,
We shimmy, shake, and steal the show.
Each joke a spark, each wink a flame,
This awkward dance, oh, what a game!

Secrets Told in Sips of Wine

In fruity sips we find our way,
Your clumsy charm brightens the day.
Pour one more, let's laugh and dine,
Each drink reveals a cheeky sign.

With every toast, a secret shared,
Our tipsy tales, they're never spared.
You spill some wine, I spill my heart,
This giggly mess is where we start.

Emotions Unfolding Like Petals

Like petals soft, our feelings bloom,
In goofy stunts, we chase the gloom.
You say a joke, I snort the tea,
Life's a circus, just you and me.

With every tickle, new heights we reach,
Your playful ways, they kindly teach.
We twirl through life, the world a stage,
In this odd play, we steal the page.

Euphoria Beneath the Blue Sky

Under the sun, we're a silly pair,
Chasing clouds without a care.
You trip on jokes, I dance on puns,
Laughter echoes like playful runs.

Ice cream melts on our noses bright,
Two clowns in love, oh what a sight!
We juggle feelings and quirky dreams,
In this circus, nothing's as it seems.

In the Stillness of a Shared Silence

Silence wraps us in a cozy hug,
While your tummy grumbles, oh so snug.
I dare not laugh, lest you see me grin,
A battle of wits we both can't win.

Your gaze like a puzzle, mixed-up and sweet,
I read your thoughts, but can't find your feet.
In this quiet, our hearts hold a tune,
A symphony played by the light of the moon.

Drenched in the Glow of Meaning

Your smile shines bright like a neon sign,
A beacon of love that feels so divine.
With every wink, I lose my place,
Drenched in your charms, I'm floating in space.

We sip on tea, but giggle like fools,
Making messes as we break all the rules.
In this chaos, we find our groove,
Two dorks in a bubble — come on, let's move!

Tidal Waves of Uncertainty

Riding the waves of what if and maybe,
A dance on the shore, but it's getting wavy.
You ask for a kiss, but then pull back quick,
Your teasing moves just make me sick!

In the swirl of confusion, we laugh and play,
Like kids in a tide pool, splashing away.
We surf through the chaos, on love's funny ride,
With each wave of doubt, we'll just stick by side.

The Sweet Scent of Possibility

In a garden of giggles, love blooms wide,
Where butterflies chat and blushing tongues hide.
Each glance a mischief, a spark in the air,
Like candy-flavored wishes that dance everywhere.

Two hearts collide over spilled soda pop,
With laughter erupting, we just can't stop.
Like shoes out of sync on a whimsical spree,
We'll trip on our dreams, so let's wait and see.

A wink is exchanged, a sigh in the breeze,
While squirrels gossip secrets among the trees.
Chasing our shadows, we spin round and round,
In this playful romance, true joy can be found.

Flickering Candles and Unsaid Dreams

Candlelight flickers, casting odd shapes,
As we giggle and make silly mistakes.
With whispers of wishes just waiting to bloom,
We're treading on air, in this cozy little room.

You joke about muffins, I can't help but tease,
While frosting my thoughts on a donut with ease.
As laughter confesses what words can't declare,
Our hearts take the stage in this twilight affair.

Each moment a spark, like fireflies' flight,
We're dancing on wishes, igniting the night.
In shadows we linger, in light we take flight,
With flickering candles, we're lost in delight.

Hearts Adrift in Celestial Whirlwinds

Oh, the stars are giggling, they wink and they sway,
As we spin on this merry-go-round of 'hey!'
With planets high-fiving and comets that kiss,
It's a cosmic joke that we simply can't miss.

Our hearts take the plunge in this meteor shower,
Creating new rhythms with magical power.
Through nebulae wild, we sail side by side,
On this cosmic carousel, there's nowhere to hide.

With stardust confetti, we twirl and we spin,
Each laughter like music, invites us to grin.
In this celestial dance, so carefree and light,
Our hearts drift like balloons, floating into the night.

A Breeze Carrying Soft Yearnings

In the breeze there's a joke that whispers 'hello',
As leaves join the laughter, a fluttering show.
Each sigh rides the wind, a feathered delight,
Our hearts like two kites, soaring high in the light.

We chase after rumors of love on the run,
With daisies debating who's having more fun.
The sun winks at us with a warm glowing face,
As butterflies dance, in this joyful embrace.

With summer's sweet breath, we sway and we sway,
A flurry of giggles to brighten our day.
In the softest of whispers, the world comes alive,
With hearts in the breeze, who needs to arrive?

The Taste of First Affection

In the cafe where laughter flows,
I dropped my fries, and so it goes.
You laughed so loud, I spilled my drink,
And suddenly, we shared a wink.

You said, "Is this your secret plan?
To charm me with your clumsy hand?"
With every smile, we stole the show,
As jellybeans rolled down below.

Petals Caught in a Gentle Wind

We danced on sidewalks, what a sight!
Your hat flew off, oh what a fright!
With petals swirling through the air,
We giggled, trying not to care.

You caught my eyes with a goofy grin,
As daisies tumbled, we fell in.
The breeze was wild, our hearts took flight,
In that silly moment, everything felt right.

The Melody of Us in Quiet Spaces

In a library, secrets shared,
I whispered jokes; you were unprepared.
The librarian shushed our delight,
As we contained our laughter tight.

You hummed a tune, but missed the beat,
I clapped my hands, couldn't stay discreet.
With every note, our hearts did sway,
In a symphony made of wordplay.

Caressed by Autumn's Cool Breath

The leaves were crisp, a crunchy treat,
We chased squirrels and danced on our feet.
You slipped on mush, did an awkward twist,
I nearly fell, you waved your fist.

"Be careful!" came a shout from afar,
As we laughed under the pumpkin star.
With cheeks aglow and spirits high,
We made our own autumn sky."

Velvet Petals and Open Secrets

In a garden where laughter does sprout,
Two roses are whispering, full of doubt.
"Do you think he's trimmed?" the pink one asked,
While the red one giggled, her petals unmasked.

Bees buzzed by, playing matchmaker's game,
With honeyed words, they aimed to inflame.
"He's dashing! He's bold!" the bluebell did sing,
While the daisies danced, gossiping 'bout spring.

The Dance of Dappled Shadows

In the moonlit grove where shadows prance,
Squirrels twirled, giving romance a chance.
A couple of owls on a branch quite askew,
Kept hooting sweet nothings, the whole night through.

The fireflies joined with a twinkling delight,
Drawing hearts in the air, glowing soft and bright.
"Who knew love could spark in such simple ways?"
Chirped a chipmunk, entranced in a daze.

Sunkissed Secrets at Dusk

As the sun dipped low, casting shadows so bold,
Two sunflowers giggled, their stories untold.
"Did you see him? The one with the bee?"
"No, but I heard he's picked up some glee!"

The crickets began their jubilant song,
With each chirp and buzz, it felt so right, so wrong.
A ladybug blushed, wings trembling with cheer,
"Love is like pollen, it's messy but dear!"

Fragrant Promises in Bloom

In a field where the daisies all wink with delight,
A daffodil shouted, "Let's plan for tonight!"
"A date? With whom?" asked the shy lavender,
"She's a whirlwind of petals! A real game changer!"

As the pansies pondered in shades of bright hue,
The wind brought sweet secrets, as breezes do.
"Let's all dress up in aromas divine,
And toast to the blooms who think they can shine!"

Serendipity's Sweet Serenade

In a café, I spilled my tea,
You laughed, and oh, what glee!
With sugar snatched from my hand,
We planned a heist, a coffee band.

Your eyes sparkled, my cheeks were red,
Our topics ranged from fish to bread.
We swapped stories like kids at play,
Chasing the mundane blues away.

Chocolate croissants, we split in halves,
With silly jokes and goofy laughs.
You tossed a napkin, it flew wide,
And with each smile, more joy inside.

So here's to chance and fortune's grin,
When hearts collide, let loves begin.
In clumsy dances, we find our beat,
In every accidental meet!

When Hands Brush and Worlds Collide

In the park, our hands drew near,
A gentle touch, a thrilling fear.
You said, 'Oops!' I said, 'Not quite!'
We giggled under the moonlit night.

Your fries were stolen, oh what fun!
French-fried romance, just begun.
With ketchup kisses and playful bites,
Every moment, a sweet delight.

Spinning in circles on the grass,
You tangled my hair, oh what sass!
With silly twirls, we danced like fools,
Breaking all the boring rules.

As laughter echoed through the trees,
We caught the whispers of the breeze.
When worlds collide and hearts entwine,
We find connection, oh so fine!

Golden Moments of Connection

Under the sun, with ice cream cones,
You dripped some down my favorite stones.
A sticky mess, but who would care?
We laughed and danced without a care.

You told a joke about a cat,
I snorted loud, imagine that!
With laughter ringing, our spirits high,
We painted rainbows across the sky.

From silly selfies to playful sighs,
We captured moments, you and I.
With every glance, a spark ignites,
In this wild world of pure delights.

So here's to moments, bright and bold,
In golden rays, our story told.
Through every laugh, we dare to dream,
Together, we make the perfect team!

Soft Shadows and Shared Dreams

Beneath the stars, we made a pact,
No serious talks, just fun and act.
With secret whispers, we shared our schemes,
And wove our futures in delightful dreams.

Your shadow danced, it looked like mine.
We two were silly, oh so divine.
With each shared giggle, the night took flight,
In soft shadows, everything felt right.

We traded tales of frogs and bees,
With goofy faces and silly pleas.
In playful jests, we found our groove,
Director's cut of a spontaneous move!

So let's keep dreaming, you and I,
In laughter's glow, the stars way up high.
Through every chuckle, a bond we weave,
In soft shadows, we truly believe!

Sun-drenched Whispers of Tomorrow

Under the sun, we played the fool,
With ice cream smiles, we broke the rule.
You with your hat, all crooked and wild,
I laughed so hard, a giddy child.

Our shadows danced, in playful haste,
Like kids at heart, no time to waste.
You tripped a bit and fell on the grass,
I couldn't help but giggle—I have no class!

The sun dipped low, sparking our dreams,
While giggling softly in moonlight beams.
Your silly jokes, my heart's delight,
Just two star-crazed fools under the night.

With whispers shared so carefree and light,
Two goofballs blending, oh what a sight!
Tomorrow's promise, we'll laugh some more,
In a world of joy, forever explore.

Fields of Enchantment and You.

In fields of green, we skipped and danced,
Your playful grin got me entranced.
You twirled like a dandelion spun,
I chased the wind; oh, what fun!

You wore those shoes, two sizes too big,
Stumbling around, like a little pig!
We laughed till we cried, our hearts so bold,
In this wild world, our love took hold.

Butterflies giggled, they joined the fun,
As you tried to catch one, and fell for the sun.
Rolling in clover, life felt so free,
In those silly moments, just you and me.

We painted the sky with colors so bright,
Each silly wink, a spark of delight.
In the fields where enchantment blooms,
Our laughter echoes like joyous tunes.

Whispers of Autumn's Embrace

Leaves fell in whirlwinds, colors ablaze,
You kicked a pile; what a clumsy craze!
With apples so shiny, we'd munch and nibble,
Sharing sweet treats—the perfect giggle.

You wore that scarf, so bundled and snug,
No fashion sense, just a cozy hug.
We leaped in the air, like kids on a spree,
Your laughter mixed with the rustling tree.

Pumpkin spice lattes we clutched with glee,
As squirrels rolled past—oh, can you see?
With each little glance, heartbeats race,
Autumn's charm in a fading embrace.

So here's to the chill, the giggles galore,
To whispered secrets and open doors.
In every moment, together we dance,
Finding the joy in our silly romance.

The Sweetness of Unspoken Words

In quiet corners, our eyes collide,
A wink here and there, nothing to hide.
Your smirk is the code that makes me grin,
In the sweetness found deep within.

We share shy glances, like secretive spies,
Who needs grand speeches or fancy goodbyes?
With each wordless laugh, love's legend grows,
In the sweetness of silence, the heart just knows.

You spill your drink, oh what a scene!
I offer napkins—both giggles and cream.
With tiny blunders, our moments expand,
Creating a world only we understand.

In the art of laughter, our spirits fly,
Through unspoken words, together we try.
So let's raise a toast to the joy that we find,
In the sweetness of moments, you're always on my mind.

Whispers of Autumn's Embrace

Leaves are falling, what a sight,
Squirrels plotting, love's delight.
Pumpkin spice in every air,
Do you think they make a pair?

Acorns tumble, hearts do race,
Chipmunks dance, they find their place.
Sweaters tight, we cozy up,
Hot cocoa spills in my cup.

Bonfire's glow, a wink or two,
Marshmallows roasted, who knew?
We laugh 'til stomachs start to ache,
That's the warmth that we now bake!

Autumn's glow, a cheeky rise,
Crisp of air, beneath the skies.
With every crunch beneath our feet,
Our hearts seem light, oh what a feat!

The Sweetness of Unspoken Words

In crowded rooms, we brush and slide,
Like secret whispers, hearts collide.
A sideways glance, a hint of cheer,
What's left unsaid hangs in the air.

Tongue-tied poets, can't find rhyme,
But there's a spark, it feels divine.
Chocolate cake and jokes shared wide,
Who needs to speak when smiles reside?

Late-night chats with bites and sips,
A chocolate melt, we steal our trips.
Between the giggles and the grins,
Unspoken love just softly spins.

Hints and nudges, fun absurd,
In every silence, sweetness stirred.
With laughter tossed like candy sprinkles,
We taste the joy, love's little twinkles!

Harvest Moonlit Serenade

Under the stars, we swing and sway,
Old tunes play in a jovial way.
Dancing shadows, laughter beams,
The moon's our ally for silly schemes.

Fingers fumble, a clumsy twirl,
We nearly trip, but then we whirl.
Corn mazes lead us here and there,
But hearts don't mind, they're in midair.

Crickets sing, a serenade sweet,
While pumpkins plot a dating feat.
With every stomp and clumsy shake,
Joy collides in laughter we make!

As moonlight paints a dreamlike scheme,
We find our way, or so we dream.
Beneath the harvest, a chance, a glance,
Fall's funny ways in our moonlit dance!

Tasting the Nectar of Affection

Sweet nectar drips from fingers gold,
Every bite, a tale retold.
Honey drizzles as we share,
Sticky fingers, love in the air.

Fruit baskets filled to the brim,
As tastes collide, our hopes begin.
Grapes of laughter, berries of fun,
We nourish joy, two hearts that run.

Pies cooling on a window sill,
Every slice, a heart to fill.
Cherry glimmers with a wink,
While warm aromas make us think.

Challenge me now, let's bake a cake,
Who knew this love could be such a bake?
With every nibble and playful tease,
We find our flavor, a taste to please!

Love's Palette Paints the Evening Sky

When hearts do dance in colors bright,
Two clumsy fools in love's delight.
In every shade, a giggle grows,
Where laughter colors where affection flows.

A splash of blue, a hint of red,
Like awkward hugs, and laughter spread.
With every brush, a silly mess,
In love's odd art, we find success.

We paint the moon with laughter loud,
And dance beneath a giggling cloud.
As shadows blend and spirits soar,
Who knew romance could be such a chore?

In the gallery of silly dreams,
Where love is more than just what seems.
A canvas streaked with sweet embrace,
In every smile, we find our place.

The Canvas of a Stolen Glance

Her eyes met mine, a fleeting spark,
Like socks that vanish in the dark.
At lunch we share a silly grin,
A symmetric chaos we dive in.

The sandwich drops, we laugh and flail,
As mustard smears an epic tale.
In crowded rooms, your gaze locks tight,
A canvas made for clumsy flight.

We scribble hearts on coffee cups,
While giggles erupt and never stop.
In secret notes, we play our game,
Two silly souls without a shame.

The world's a stage for love's charade,
In stolen glances, bliss conveyed.
With every smile, and every chance,
We paint a life of clumsy romance.

Tender Moments in Fleeting Time

Two hearts collide in awkward spins,
Like tangled sheets with no clear wins.
With wobbly steps, we start to sway,
In clumsy love, we find our way.

A moment brief, a silly twirl,
Your hair's a mess, and so's my world.
We share a laugh, and time stands still,
In tangled feet, we find the thrill.

The clock ticks loud, yet hours flee,
What's love, if not pure entropy?
In every blink, a spark we chase,
Each stolen moment, a silly embrace.

Through fleeting days, we laugh aloud,
Two dorks in love, forever proud.
We may trip often, but that's just fine,
In all the chaos, you still are mine.

Gravity of Hearts Colliding

When gravity pulls with awkward grace,
Two hearts collide, a silly race.
We bounce like balls in empty space,
A cosmic dance, a cheeky chase.

With goofy smiles, we trip and fall,
In every stumble, we hear love's call.
The universe laughs, spins us tight,
As hearts collide in joyful flight.

A serenade of clumsy laughs,
With silly jokes about our paths.
In orbit, we find our own sweet beat,
Two gravity-bound souls, so neat.

We spin and twirl, a crazy waltz,
In every fumble, love's the pulse.
So here's to us, the oddest two,
In every collision, a love so true.

The Threads of Connection

In a café, you spill your drink,
I laugh so hard, I start to blink.
A napkin note, you try to write,
But doodles make the moment light.

You trip on air, my heart takes flight,
As laughter lifts us both that night.
Our clumsy words, a sweet ballet,
Creating laughs, come what may.

We swap our snacks, a silly trade,
Your head's in clouds, I'm in the shade.
Under neon lights, we share our dreams,
Who knew love's brewed in awkward schemes?

With every giggle, sparks are sown,
In this café, we're not alone.
Uneven steps, and jokes we spin,
Two hearts linked by a flirty grin.

An Ode to Fleeting Glances

From across the street, a wink, a grin,
You catch my gaze, and my cheeks begin.
A fleeting spark, a moment shared,
Your silly hat, I can't help but stare.

The wind plays tricks, your hair takes flight,
I laugh and wave, feeling quite light.
Our eyes collide, like two wayward darts,
Oh, these quick moments, they steal our hearts.

In crowded rooms, where awkwardness blooms,
We exchange looks while dancing with brooms.
You pretend to trip, I stifle a laugh,
How can true love be just a paragraph?

Yet in each glance, a story unfolds,
Two souls entwined, defying the mold.
With every sight, a secret glance,
Together we might just take the chance.

The Intersection of Dreams and Reality

In dreams, we dance on rooftops bright,
In reality's grip, we fumble for light.
You tell a joke, the punchline falls flat,
I snort like a pig, a silly mishap.

We challenge fate, like pair of fools,
Creating memories that break the rules.
A shared sandwich, a bit too large,
Both of us taking an equal charge.

Reality checks, and we both laugh loud,
No fancy lines, just love unbowed.
We leap through puddles on this wild ride,
With each silly moment, we grow side by side.

The edge of dreams, where we both collide,
In sleep's embrace, no need to hide.
Awkward and weird, that's how it goes,
In this sweet chaos, our affection grows.

Flourishing with Anticipated Touches

A brush of hands, oh what a tease,
You giggle softly, my heart does freeze.
Spilled secrets, over cups of tea,
Every sip shared feels like a spree.

We dance around like playful mice,
Avoiding traps, oh isn't that nice?
Your laugh is music, a catchy tune,
My heart is strumming under the moon.

Butterflies flutter, both tame and bold,
Whispers of stories waiting to be told.
With each small touch, excitement grows,
In the garden of flirtation, love sows.

So here we stand, with shy little grins,
Both nervous souls, where fun begins.
Anticipation hangs thick in the air,
In this hilarity, we make the perfect pair.

Unfolding Like a Love Letter

He wrote me a note, oh so sweet,
With doodles of hearts and a lunch to eat.
But the ink was blue, and my coffee's black,
Now I sip and wonder, did I sign the pact?

I asked him to dance, he tripped on air,
He spun like a top, with floppy hair.
Our feet tangled tight, we laughed out loud,
As the cat skulked by, feeling all proud.

He sent me a text, full of memes,
Said, "Let's meet at noon, no more daydreams!"
But he mixed up the time, I sat and I fumed,
While he twirled in circles, my patience consumed.

Yet through the blunders, my heart took flight,
In every giggle, things felt just right.
With each little mishap, we keep on growing,
Falling for you, my sweet, clumsy showing.

The Glimmer of Sunset Promises

We watched the sun dip, a buttery ball,
He tripped on his words, then nearly on me.
His ice cream cone slipped, what a sticky fall,
But we laughed like fools, all carefree.

The sky blushed red, we made silly vows,
To always eat dessert before dinner, somehow.
His pinky's on mine, like a tangled string,
While we giggle and munch — love's peculiar fling.

Fireflies danced, like they knew our plans,
He waved a bug off, while munching on yams.
With a wink and a smile, under stars up high,
We called out to Cupid; hope he heard our sighs.

As twilight whispers sweet nonsense in ears,
We hide our laughter, we hide our fears.
With each moment shared, a sparkle awakes,
In flavors of laughter, my heart gently quakes.

Between Colliding Seasons

Spring sent me flowers, bright and absurd,
He brought me a cactus, it really got spurred.
With colors so vibrant, we fit like a tune,
While dodging the pollen, true love's a boon.

Summer arrived, and we jumped in the pool,
He cannonballed first, acting like a fool.
My splashes were weak, but my laughter was loud,
While our clothes on the grass formed a drying crowd.

Autumn fell softly, with leaves in a dance,
We built a small fort, took a playful chance.
But there came a squirrel, looking for snacks,
As we rolled on the floor, dodging little attacks.

And winter now whispers, with flurries of snow,
We sip on hot chocolate, hearts all aglow.
Each season collides, like dreams all around,
In the funny little moments, love can be found.

The Harvest of Our Heartstrings

In the orchard we strolled, plucking ripe fruit,
He called me a peach, best joke of the suit.
I tossed him an apple, it fell on his toe,
But we laughed like mad, with a playful "whoa!"

With baskets in hand, we danced in the sun,
He spun like a whirlwind, arms out for fun.
He stumbled on pumpkins, fell flat on the ground,
Yet from laughter's abyss, a sweet love was found.

The cider was bubbling, we toasted and cheered,
To the messes we made, our hearts never feared.
In the sweetness of harvest, we picked out our fate,
With each cackle shared, it was never too late.

Now each fruit on the tree, a tale to retell,
Of romance so juicy, we fell under its spell.
In the laughter and giggles, the joy we can cling,
Life's silly little harvest brings love as our ring.

Nature's Chorus of Togetherness

In the garden we giggle, butterflies applaud,
Chasing each other, we trip like a clod.
Bees buzz conspiracies, flowers sway in cheer,
Whispers of love bloom, loud enough to hear.

Squirrels throw nuts like love notes in jest,
Each acorn a beacon, a nutty request.
The sun paints our cheeks with a cheeky grin,
As laughter finds roots in the chaos within.

Birds hop around, they join our delight,
Flapping their wings, they dance in plain sight.
We share our snacks, a picnic so sweet,
Even ants make it over to join this feast.

Nature's own jesters, they sing in the breeze,
With playful antics that aim to please.
In this playful realm, with hearts open wide,
We toast to the fun of this countryside ride.

Entwined in a Tapestry of Light

Under twinkling stars, we spin like a top,
Falling and laughing, we can't seem to stop.
With moonlight as friends, we sway to the sound,
In this silly waltz, love's lost and all found.

Fireflies flicker, like fairies on cue,
They tag our wishes, the old and the new.
Umbrellas of giggles cover all that we've lost,
In this dance of delight, we count up the cost.

A blanket of laughter wraps tight around us,
With each silly whisper, there's no need to fuss.
As we trip on our dreams, the night doesn't care,
Entwined in the joy, we float up in air.

This tapestry glows, a dance of the sun,
Fingers entwined, two hearts on the run.
With every bright shimmer, let joy be our guide,
In this crazy quilt, let's tumble and slide.

The Last Dance of Summer's Flame

Summer's last hug brings a wiggly cheer,
With the heat of the day, we twirl without fear.
Ice creams are dripping, slipping right down,
As we laugh and skewer the town like a clown.

The sun dips low, a fiery surprise,
While I try to catch you with narrowed-down eyes.
You dodge and you weave, like a dancer in flight,
Spinning through twilight, turning wrong into right.

With sneakers that squeak, we moonwalk through grass,
No rhythm or rhyme, we don't need the class.
We throw caution to winds, like kites on the run,
In this last dance, it's just you, me, and fun.

As the shadows grow longer, we chuckle and sway,
Wrapped in the warmth of a perfect day.
So here's to the blaze that lights up our way,
In summer's last dance, let's laugh and display.

Against the Backdrop of Falling Leaves

Leaves swirl around like confetti of cheer,
As we leap into piles, free of all fear.
Our laughter ignites like the crisp autumn air,
Squirrelly encounters, our hearts laid bare.

With each crunchy step, we shuffle and slide,
Dressed up in sweaters, the world as our guide.
A dance of the branches, the sky laughs with us,
In this silly ballet, there's simply no fuss.

Pumpkins grin wide, oh what a delight,
We make silly faces, with joy taking flight.
As the world turns golden, we frolic and play,
Each spin through the leaves brightens up our day.

Against falling blooms, love's funny refrain,
Bringing us closer, through sunshine and rain.
As autumn blows kisses, we giggle with glee,
In this seasonal dance, just you and me.

Chasing After Stars Together

We lay on grass, our backs to earth,
Counting constellations, each one a mirth.
You nudged me hard, said I missed a flash,
I pointed back, claiming I was brash.

A shooting star zipped through the dark,
You made a wish for a pet goldfish, a lark.
I chuckled hard, thinking of the pond,
We dreamt of fish that could wave and respond.

With cosmic maps scribbled on our knees,
We debated names for galactic cheese.
You swore you saw a comet, but it was a fly,
Laughter erupted, oh my, oh my!

As starlight twinkled in mischievous ways,
We crafted stories to fill the gray days.
Under the blanket of infinite bliss,
I knew right then, I couldn't miss this.

Vibrations in the Quiet Air

On a bench we sat, strumming time's tune,
You plucked a note that shaped the balloon.
I laughed out loud, it squeaked in reply,
Like lovebirds whispering, oh my, oh my!

A breeze danced by, tickling the trees,
We shared silly jokes that got lost in the breeze.
Your face turned bright, a reflection of glee,
Who knew romance could start with a 'hee-hee'?

Invisible rhythms floated around,
As we invented dances to nowhere bound.
You twirled and stumbled, your shoelace became
A handle for laughter that cracked like a frame.

In these quiet moments, connections blew near,
With every giggle, our worries disappeared.
Like silly magnets, we gravitated close,
Bound by a humor that nobody knows.

Pathways Woven with Sweet Intentions

We strip the map, let spontaneity guide,
With candy in pocket, we strolled side by side.
You pointed to puddles, claiming they'd yield,
Adventures in rain, like a mental field.

With every step, plans twisted and twirled,
You dared me to dance, I boldly whirled.
We tripped over laughter, our shoes went astray,
Puddles splashed us as we danced all day.

Finding footprints that looked quite absurd,
We followed them, giggling, not saying a word.
Each signpost a riddle, each turn a delight,
With chocolate bars swapped for moonlight so bright.

At the end of the path, a café appeared,
We shared chilly shakes, both cold and weird.
"Two straws, one cup," you slyly declared,
I smiled in wonder, feeling quite bared.

The Garden of Passion's Bloom

In a garden where daisies giggle so bright,
We planted our secrets beneath the moonlight.
You shouted, "These bulbs are more than they seem!"
I said, "Let's water them with goofy esteem!"

A bouquet of blunders grew tall and proud,
Each petal a chuckle, a fruit of the crowd.
You claimed a rose starts as a spinster's plight,
'Till bees come to tease it, it's quite a fright!

With watering cans full of silly, we knew,
Our plot flourished wildly with jokes that felt new.
Sunflowers winked, while violets professed,
We vowed to come back and give them our best.

In the warm glow of twilight's embrace,
We nibbled on petals, sharing good grace.
Oh, the secrets we'd whispered beneath leafy boughs,
In our humorous garden, love took its vows.

Unraveled Threads of Intimacy

In mismatched socks, we roam the floor,
With playful nudges, we explore.
A pizza slice, a shared delight,
You wink and say, "I'll take a bite!"

Your coffee's cold, while mine's too hot,
I spill it all; oh, what a plot!
You laugh and sigh, then take my hand,
In this crazy world, we take our stand.

We bicker over who left the mess,
Yet yo-yo kisses lead to happiness.
With every quirk and little grind,
We make our way, just love defined.

So let's untangle all we can,
With silly talks from this sweet man.
In every silly, sweet charade,
Our love is like a fun parade.

The Language of Gentle Touches

A playful poke, a teasing jab,
Your tickles make me laugh and grab.
In secret notes, our jokes reside,
With every giggle, we take a ride.

When hands collide in clumsy dance,
You spin me 'round, I lose my chance.
With silly steps, we twirl and sway,
In every touch, love finds its play.

We speak in winks and silly grins,
As laughter bubbles, the merriment wins.
In fleeting glances, a spark ignites,
Every moment, our love incites.

So here's to you, my goofy friend,
With every touch, our hearts transcend.
In this funny language, we perfectly blend,
Forever together, on you I depend.

Vibrant Hues of Courting

Your socks are bright, a rainbow's dream,
While I trip over my own scheme.
We mix our colors like a child,
In this palette, our hearts run wild.

In board games where we both compete,
You claim your win, I take a seat.
We laugh till we cry, it's pure delight,
In painted moments, our hearts ignite.

With laughter loud, we splatter paint,
From fairytales, we love, no restraint.
You draw a heart, I scribble mine,
In vibrant hues, we intertwine.

So let's canvas life, both bright and fun,
In this playful art, we've just begun.
With every splash, our love's a song,
In this crazy world, we both belong.

Timeless Tides of Togetherness

On sandy shores, we build and play,
You splash water, I try to stay.
With laughter rolling like the waves,
Together, love misbehaves.

We race the tide, we skip on shells,
In goofy glee, our laughter swells.
I catch a crab, you scream and run,
In this ocean, we've just begun.

As sunsets glow, we share a snack,
You sneak a chip, I sneak it back.
In salty breezes, we dance with glee,
In waves of love, just you and me.

So here's to tides that rise and fall,
With every splash, we hear the call.
In timeless moments, we craft our bliss,
In every wave, I find your kiss.

The Promise Written in Summer's Breath

In the park where laughter plays,
Two ducks dance in silly ways.
A sunburned clown juggles pies,
While kids burst forth with squeaky cries.

Beneath the trees, a shy glance shared,
As ice cream drips, nobody's scared.
A butterfly lands on my nose,
We both laugh, oh how time goes!

In warm sunlight, secrets hide,
With flip-flops on, we take a ride.
A picnic basket, crumbs galore,
We munch and giggle, asking for more.

When summer fades, we'll look back,
On silly days, our hearts won't lack.
With memories sweet, just like pie,
We'll fondly chuckle as days fly by.

Moonlit Paths and Hidden Hopes

In the moonlight, shadows prance,
A cat sneezes, gives us a chance.
Two shadows linger on a bench,
As we whisper, and thoughts clench.

The stars wink at every word,
While laughter dances, barely heard.
A squirrel skitters, steals a scene,
With his nutty antics, a furry glean.

With each step, we share a laugh,
Unruly socks, a silly gaffe.
I trip and splash in puddles deep,
You snicker, and my heart takes leap.

Our dreams alight like fireflies,
In hidden hopes, where laughter lies.
The moon, a witness to our spree,
With every slip, you cherish me.

When Eyes Lock and Hearts Race

Across the room, I catch your stare,
You wink, then fumble, oh how rare!
A drink spills down your pristine shirt,
As laughter erupts, it's quite the flirt.

Each awkward pause, a spark ignites,
Like two clumsy stars on dizzy flights.
You grin as I trip on my own feet,
An epic fail, but oh, so sweet!

In crowded places, we find our spot,
You play it cool, but it's quite hot.
The air is thick with silly vibes,
As we mix truth with playful jibes.

A sudden bump, our drinks collide,
A sticky moment, but full of pride.
When eyes lock tight, the world's a blur,
With laughter echoing, hearts confer!

A Symphony of Entwined Souls

With strings of fate, our laughter plays,
In mischief's tune, we'll dance for days.
A kazoo's sound, it fills the air,
As melodies twist with flair and care.

In cans of soda, bubbles fizz,
Our jokes fly by, like shooting whiz.
With every note, we take our stand,
Crafting silly dreams, oh so grand!

A trumpet blares, the whole crowd sways,
We giggle and twirl in rhythmic ways.
As laughter becomes our magic spell,
In the symphony, we ring the bell.

In tangled hearts, our music grows,
With silly solos, everyone knows.
Together we sway, two souls in time,
Playing this life, our silly rhyme.

The Dance of Two Hearts Beating

He stepped on her toes with flair,
She giggled, what a clumsy pair.
They twirled like leaves in autumn's breeze,
Two hearts in chaos, both at ease.

With every spin, a laugh would burst,
He claims he's good; she quells the thirst.
They dance under a disco ball,
Echoes of laughter, love's sweet call.

His moves are wild, hers are refined,
They shimmy through the night, entwined.
A jive that's wacky, far from neat,
Yet, what a joy, their own heartbeat!

So let them sway, with silly grace,
In this fun dance, they take their place.
Two hearts collide, such perfect bliss,
In every giggle, a stolen kiss.

Savoring the Juices of Affection

A picnic spread with treats galore,
He squished a peach; it rolled on the floor.
She laughed so hard, she couldn't breathe,
As juice dripped down like sweet reprieve.

They munched on cherries, juicy and bold,
With every bite, more stories told.
He wore a halo of sticky jam,
While she just giggled, 'Oh, what a man!'

The watermelon was far too big,
He tried to lift it, did a jig.
With laughter ringing through the air,
They savored fruits, without a care.

In every bite, a spark ignites,
Two jokers dancing under sunlight.
With every morsel, love's duet,
In sticky sweetness, no regret.

Sweet Serenades Under the Stars

In the moonlight, he struck a chord,
Her off-key voice was quite adored.
They sang of love in silly tones,
While serenading, knocking over phones.

His guitar's missing a string or two,
Yet she hums along, her heart so true.
A ballad old, now freshly sung,
With every note, their love is flung.

They danced like dorks beneath the sky,
A twinkle in her hazel eye.
With crickets chirping their sweet refrain,
The stars applauded their joyful pain.

So here they are, two hearts a'blaze,
Making music, lost in a daze.
With laughter echoing through the night,
Their love is quirky, yet feels so right.

Where Passion Meets the Glistening Shore

On sandy shores, they built a mound,
A castle made, but then it drowned.
The waves tickled their silly feet,
As they giggled, feeling the heat.

He playfully splashed, she squealed out loud,
A jubilant couple, far from proud.
The sunset painted a canvas bright,
With laughter weaving their hearts in light.

A seagull swooped, stole their fries,
They chased it down, full of surprise.
Today's affair, so wild and free,
With salty kisses by the sea.

So let them frolic, let them play,
Two souls entwined in a sunny ballet.
With every wave, their love will soar,
A humorous tale on the sandy shore.

A Blossom in the Gentle Breeze

You caught my eye like a blooming flower,
Your smile, a petal, makes the sun cower.
We danced through fields where the daisies play,
But you tripped on a root, oh what a display!

Your laugh is like honey, sweet and bright,
I swear it could charm even the moon at night.
Yet, when you sought to impress with a twirl,
You spun like a top and fell, oh what a whirl!

The bees buzz around, hear our giggles soar,
I'd say it's romantic, but you snore and roar.
A picnic spread wide under skies so blue,
Then you dropped the sandwiches, what a debut!

Still, in every moment, my heart sings a tune,
With you, even mishaps feel like a boon.
So here's to the fun, the laughter we share,
Like blossoms in spring, we make quite the pair.

Citrus Kisses and Starlit Nights

We met at a party, so loud and bright,
You slipped on a peel, oh what a sight!
Your laughter rang out, like a bell so clear,
Had me chuckling while I nursed my beer.

Your jokes were as tangy as solar flares,
Each punchline a twist, caught my heart unwares.
We strolled through the dark, with stars overhead,
You told me I'm zesty, to your lime spread.

We shared citrus kisses, sticky and sweet,
As fruit flies joined in, we laughed at the feat.
A lemon-themed dance? Oh, what a scene!
You attempted a twist, fell down on your bean!

Still, it was magic, under this cosmic show,
With each little hiccup, my heart's all aglow.
Here's to the laughter, the quirky delight,
Just you and me, on this zesty night!

Cherries in the Twilight

We met by a tree, where the cherries grew,
You winked at me slyly, oh what a view!
We plucked at the fruit, with a mischievous grin,
But you tossed a few, oh where did they spin?

I laughed as they splattered, the juice made a scene,
You said, 'This is romance?' with a charming sheen.
But your cheeks they turned red, like summer's best berry,

And I knew right then, this would not be scary.

We danced on the grass with our sticky hands,
Each step was a giggle, like two teenage bands.
An impromptu soirée, under twilight's gleam,
With cherries all over, we burst into scream!

So here's to our jokes, and the sweetness we share,
With laughter and fruit, we make quite the pair.
In these silly moments, my heart takes its flight,
With you, my dear friend, it feels just so right!

Swaying Hearts Under Dappled Sunlight

In a meadow of daisies, we stumbled and fell,
Your hat flew away, oh what a swell!
You laughed like a child, with your hair all a mess,
And I popped a balloon, much to my distress.

We danced through the sunshine, our shadows did play,
Through dappled trees, giggling all the day.
Your twinkle-toe steps sent butterflies soaring,
But tripping on roots left us both adoring.

With cookies and lemonade, we made quite the spread,
Until ants stole our snack, and we both fled.
Yet amidst all the chaos, my heart did one flip,
As you tossed me a wink and a playful quip.

So here's to the laughter, the fun we create,
Each mishap together feels like fate.
In swaying green fields, love grows without fright,
With you, my sweet partner, all's sunny and bright!

The Fire Beneath the Longing

In the kitchen, hearts will brew,
Spices dancing, simmering too.
I drop my spoon, it clatters loud,
You laugh and say, "Why not be proud?"

Flavors mix like love's sweet dance,
A pinch of hope, a dash of chance.
You spill the beans, I spill my tea,
We're both a little clumsy, you see.

Music of the Whispering Leaves

Underneath the leafy trees,
Your laughter floats upon the breeze.
A squirrel scurries, steals our sight,
You squeal, "He wants a date tonight!"

We shimmy close, a dance so bold,
Like secret notes that weren't foretold.
A tap, a twirl, we spin around,
Till we trip over roots in the ground.

A Kaleidoscope of Heartfelt Wishes

In a world of colorful dreams,
You wink and share absurd themes.
From magic beans to flying cows,
Our giggles echo, oh, the hows!

A tapestry of silly hopes,
We build with laughter, stretching ropes.
Your eyes are stars, they twinkle bright,
Together, we craft the weirdest flight.

The Taste of Honeyed Memories

A jar of honey on the shelf,
I ponder love and myself.
I smear it on a piece of toast,
You say, "That's how I love you most!"

Sticky fingers, sweet delight,
We giggle through the day and night.
Each memory, a treasure sweet,
Life's little bites make us complete.

Sunset Kisses on Soft Skin

As daylight fades, we chase the sun,
With giggles loud, the day feels fun.
A clumsy dance, we sway and twirl,
Your kiss, a giggle, our world a whirl.

Sunset's glow makes us feel so bold,
Our secrets shared, both new and old.
You stole my fries, I took your heart,
In this silly game, we both play a part.

Waves crash down, we laugh and splash,
A playful move, then down you crash.
Your splashy smile, a radiant sight,
In this playful dusk, everything feels right.

With sunset hues and laughter bright,
We dream of stars, just out of sight.
In our quirky ways, we intertwine,
With every kiss, I'm yours, you're mine.

In the Garden of Heartbeats

In the garden where silly flowers bloom,
We dig for laughter, dispel the gloom.
You water my dreams with pots of cheer,
With every glance, my heart draws near.

Those daisies giggle, and roses dance,
In this patch of joy, we take a chance.
With butterfly whispers and squirrel pranks,
We paint a canvas, giving love thanks.

Your puns are petals, they make me swoon,
Our hearts are beating a funny tune.
In this garden wild, we plant delight,
As every heartbeat grows through the night.

We dance with bees, shake hands with bees,
The sunbeams tell our tales with ease.
In the garden of laughter, we play the role,
With silly seeds, we grow as a whole.

Laughter Beneath the Harvest Moon

Under the moon, we skip and slide,
With jokes and jests, it's quite the ride.
You try to dance, trip on a gourd,
We laugh so hard, the smiles are stored.

Pumpkin spice makes the air sweet,
While we play tag with our two left feet.
Your wit's a treasure, a funny delight,
In this moonlit field, everything's bright.

The harvest moon winks, a sly old friend,
We share chuckles that never end.
With corny tales and snickers shared,
Each laugh, a bond, forever paired.

So let the moon shine on our fun,
With laughter echoing, two hearts as one.
In this playful night, romantically bold,
We gather the moments, like stars to hold.

Echoes of Love in Bloom

Amidst the daisies, love takes flight,
Our banter dances in morning light.
With silly faces, we flirt and tease,
In echoing laughter, we find our ease.

Your puns blossom like tulips in spring,
Each witty line makes my heart sing.
In this field of echoes, laughter spills,
With every bloom, my heart thrills.

We gather wildflowers in a silly spree,
With bee costumes and honeyed glee.
In a garden where chuckles bloom anew,
You're the punchline I always pursue.

As petals fall softly, love paints the sky,
In echoes of laughter, watch us fly.
Romance in chaos, a sweet love tune,
With echoes of joy, forever in bloom.

Delicate Threads of Connection

In a café full of chatter, laughter flies,
A wink from across the table, oh my oh my!
He spilled his drink, she feigned surprise,
Love is clumsy, but oh, it tries!

With a shared slice of cake, the frosting's a mess,
Two blushes collide, it's a humorous caress.
Their jokes fall flat, but they're still quite blessed,
In this tangled web, they both confess.

Berries and Blossoms of Belonging

In a garden of laughter, strawberries grow,
She picked one up, called it 'sour', oh no!
He jokingly claimed, 'Let's give it a throw!'
A berry fight breaks out, what a wild show!

Petals in the breeze, they dance and they swirl,
With every misstep, they giggle and twirl.
Catching fleeting glances, their hearts start to whirl,
In this fruity chaos, love starts to unfurl.

A Symphony of Summer's Glow

Under the sun's spotlight, they play in the sand,
A mix-up of towels, now isn't that grand?
She's sunburned on one side, while he's surprisingly tanned,
A symphony of mishaps, not quite what they planned.

Beach balls keep flying, they dodge and they sway,
With laughter so loud, no words go astray.
He asked her for water, she spilled it, hooray!
In this bright, silly moment, they both want to stay.

Sipping Wine Under the Blossoms

With glasses of red, they toast to the trees,
A squirrel steals a snack, oh what a tease!
She laughs so hard, she spills with ease,
Rolling on the grass, as light as a breeze.

The petals fall down like a soft, sweet rain,
He tries to catch one, but it's quite the game.
Each fumble and giggle, a joyful refrain,
Underneath the blossoms, love's silly domain.

www.ingramcontent.com/pod-product-compliance
Lightning Source LLC
Chambersburg PA
CBHW060141230426
43661CB00003B/524